We are the Brontë Sisters

adapted by Brooke Vitale

PENGUIN YOUNG READERS LICENSES
An Imprint of Penguin Random House LLC, New York

Published in 2020 by Penguin Young Readers Licenses, an imprint of Penguin Random House LLC, New York. Manufactured in China.

Visit us online at www.penguinrandomhouse.com.

ISBN 9780593096376   10 9 8 7 6 5 4 3 2 1

"Brad!" Yadina shouted. "Is it done yet?"

"We can't wait for your new Bike Man comic!" Xavier said.

Brad looked up from where he was sitting. "Prepare for disappointment."

"What's wrong, Brad?" Xavier asked, sitting down beside his friend.

Brad pointed at the half-drawn comic on his lap. "I've been thinking for days and days . . . but I can't come up with a good ending."

"No ending?" Yadina asked, sitting down, too. "Stories need an ending."

Brad sighed. "I know," he said. "But I'm out of ideas. I guess Bike Man has gone on his last ride."

Yadina jumped up. "Last ride? No way! What if Bike Man teams up with Wonder President? I, Wonder President, will join forces with Bike Man to save the world," she said, waving Brad over. "Right, Bike Man?"

"I think she wants you to pretend to be Bike Man," Xavier whispered.

Yadina nodded. "Acting it out might help you come up with an idea for your ending."

Brad shook his head. "That's not how I come up with my story ideas," he said. "I use my imagination to think up ideas in my head, then I draw them on paper." Brad looked down at his comic again. "But my imagination isn't working right now."

Xavier jumped up. "Then I guess it's time for the Secret Museum!"

The friends raced to the Secret Museum. Inside, they found three books sitting on the podium.

"*Three* artifacts?" Yadina said, looking at the books. "That's different."

Brad nodded. "Do you think one person wrote all those books? Whoever it was must have had lots of ideas!"

Brad was still looking at the books when an image of three women appeared.

"Hey, look! Charlotte, Emily, and Anne Brontë," Xavier said. "That's who we're going to meet."

"I sure hope the Brontë sisters can help you, Brad," Yadina said. "The world *needs* more Bike Man stories."

The friends placed their hands on Berby. After a great flash of light, they found themselves looking at an old stone house.

"Whoa. So this is England in 1826," Xavier said.

"Actually, you're not in England," a voice said. "You're in Glass Town."

The friends spun around. They saw three young girls. It was the Brontë sisters!

"We'll take you to the heart of Glass Town—where the fun happens," Charlotte offered.

Yadina looked at her friends and shrugged. They had been sent here for a reason. They might as well go with the girls! So Brad, Xavier, and Yadina followed them up a flight of stairs to a dusty attic.

"Welcome to . . . Glass Town," Charlotte said, throwing the door open.

"It's a town we made up ourselves," Anne explained.

"Where imaginary people live fantastical lives," Emily continued.

"And where we use our imaginations to create stories," Charlotte finished.

Xavier grinned. "I get it. It's pretend play!"

"How do you know what's going to happen in your story?" Brad asked, confused.

"We don't!" Anne said. "In pretend play, you just make up the story as you go."

Emily nodded. "And sometimes you can come up with ideas by drawing, singing, or observing the people around you . . ."

Anne jumped up. "But right now, we're using pretend play to tell the story of—"

"The circus!" Charlotte interrupted.

Emily and Anne each grabbed long poles. Holding them out, they pretended to walk across a tightrope.

Meanwhile, Charlotte handed Yadina a coat and a top hat.

Yadina happily took the costume. Putting it on, she shouted, "Welcome, everyone! I am the ringmaster."

Brad watched the imaginary circus. The Brontë sisters seemed to have a lot of ideas, but he still didn't understand how they came up with them.

"Where are these ideas coming from?" he asked.

"Pretend play gets our imaginations going," Anne said. "You should try it."

Xavier jumped up. The sisters' pretend play looked like fun. He wanted to try it, too.

"Who can I be in the circus?" he asked. "A magician? An alien? A clown? Ooooh! A magical alien clown!"

Charlotte laughed. "It's time to start the show," she said. Then, grabbing a blanket, she threw it over a pile of boxes. "Which will take place on a huge mountain!"

Brad looked at the blanket covering the pile of boxes. "That's just a pile of stuff covered by a blanket," he said, a bit confused by their game of pretend.

But his friends weren't listening.

As Brad watched, Xavier threw a long scarf on the floor. "To get there, you must cross a wobbly bridge," he said.

Yadina and the sisters nodded, then happily walked across the "bridge."

"Welcome, one and all, to the Great Mountaintop Circus!" Yadina shouted in her best ringmaster voice. "Our first act is the Terrific Tightrope Twins!"

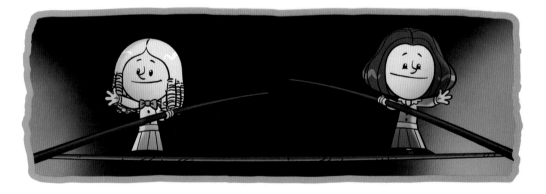

Anne and Emily stood up and spun across the pretend tightrope with flair! When they reached the other side, they bowed. Xavier, Yadina, and Charlotte cheered loudly. Brad couldn't help but smile a little.

"Next up is the Amazing Xavier: the world's first magical alien clown," Yadina announced.

"For my first trick," he said, "I'm going to make something disappear. *Alakazam, alakazoo—*"

But before he could finish, Charlotte shouted, "But then . . . disaster struck. The Amazing Xavier was a good magician. A little *too* good. He made the bridge disappear!"

Charlotte grabbed the scarf and threw it to the side. "Now everyone was stuck on the mountaintop—with no way back! If only there were a hero to rescue them. But who in Glass Town could be our hero?"

Charlotte looked at Brad, who looked down at his Bike Man comic. "Who, I say? *WHO?*" Charlotte repeated.

Brad looked back up at the circus and did a double take. The blanket-covered boxes were gone. In their place stood a real mountain. Yadina, Xavier, and the Brontë sisters had become real circus performers who were stuck and needed his help!

"However will this story end?" Charlotte cried.

"Tragically, I assume," Emily said.

But Brad was not about to let his friends down! "I am Bike Man. And I will . . . um . . ." Brad looked around the room, his imagination taking hold. ". . . I'll jump to the mountaintop to rescue you," he finished.

Brad began to pedal, and Bike Man jumped across the mountain to save his friends. Putting each one of his friends on his bike one by one, he took them to safety.

"Bike Man rescued everyone on the mountaintop," Charlotte said. "Bike Man saved the day!"

"Now *that* was a great story!" Anne said.

Emily shrugged. "Not as tragic as I expected, but a good ending."

Brad looked around the attic. The mountain was once again a pile of boxes with a blanket over it. The circus performers were just his friends again. But the magic remained. "There *are* lots of ways to come up with story ideas," he said. "And pretending to be Bike Man helped me come up with a great one!"

Brad turned to the Brontë sisters. "Charlotte? Emily? Anne? Thanks for your help. But I have to get back home to finish my own story now."

The friends waved goodbye and headed to the attic door. Berby was waiting for them. There was a great flash of light, and they found themselves back at home.

A short time later, Xavier and Yadina sat on the museum steps, listening to Brad.

"Then Bike Man rode up the hill at lightning speed to join forces with Wonder President," Brad said. "And together they stopped the evil Dr. Zoom from eating all the world's popcorn."

Xavier and Yadina jumped to their feet, clapping loudly. Brad had finished his Bike Man comic, and it was his best one yet! Even better, he knew now that there were so many ways to come up with stories, just like the Brontë sisters.